YOUNG MEN'S EDITION
MUSICAL THEATRE ANTHOLOGY FOR TEENS

COMPILED BY LOUISE LERCH

To access companion recorded
accompaniments online, visit:
www.halleonard.com/mylibrary

Enter Code
4390-6863-1382-8813

ISBN 978-0-634-04764-0

HAL•LEONARD® CORPORATION
7777 W. BLUEMOUND RD. P.O. BOX 13819 MILWAUKEE, WI 53213

For all works contained herein:
Unauthorized copying, arranging, adapting, recording or public performance is an infringement of copyright.
Infringers are liable under the law.

Visit Hal Leonard Online at
www.halleonard.com

CONTENTS

4	All Good Gifts / GODSPELL
8	All I Need Is the Girl / GYPSY
12	Any Dream Will Do / JOSEPH AND THE AMAZING TECHNICOLOR® DREAMCOAT
17	The Best Thing for You / CALL ME MADAM
20	Empty Chairs at Empty Tables / LES MISÉRABLES
26	Everybody Ought to Have a Maid / A FUNNY THING HAPPENED ON THE WAY TO THE FORUM
30	Ev'rything I've Got / BY JUPITER
38	Gaston / BEAUTY AND THE BEAST: THE BROADWAY MUSICAL
35	Gonna Build a Mountain / STOP THE WORLD—I WANT TO GET OFF
46	I Can't Stand Still / FOOTLOOSE
52	If I Can't Love Her / BEAUTY AND THE BEAST: THE BROADWAY MUSICAL
60	I'm a Bad, Bad Man / ANNIE GET YOUR GUN
64	Isn't It? / SATURDAY NIGHT
68	It's a Lovely Day Today / CALL ME MADAM
76	Kansas City / OKLAHOMA!
71	The Kite / YOU'RE A GOOD MAN, CHARLIE BROWN
82	Mama, a Rainbow / MINNIE'S BOYS
86	Mama Says / FOOTLOOSE
98	Many Moons Ago / ONCE UPON A MATTRESS
93	Me / BEAUTY AND THE BEAST: THE BROADWAY MUSICAL
107	Mister Cellophone / CHICAGO
104	Movies Were Movies / MACK AND MABEL
112	My Name / OLIVER!
118	One Song Glory / RENT
126	The Only Home I Know / SHENANDOAH
129	On the Street Where You Live / MY FAIR LADY
134	Plant a Raddish / THE FANTASTICKS
138	Razzle Dazzle / CHICAGO
144	Reviewing the Situation / OLIVER!
150	Rumble, Rumble, Rumble / THE PERILS OF PAULINE
147	Soon It's Gonna Rain / THE FANTASTICKS
156	The Tale of the Oyster / FIFTY MILLION FRENCHMEN
162	Waitin' for the Light to Shine / BIG RIVER
176	When I'm Not Near the Girl I Love / FINIAN'S RAINBOW
169	Where Was I When They Passed Out the Luck? / MINNIE'S BOYS
164	A Wonderful Day Like Today / THE ROAR OF THE GREASEPAINT—THE SMELL OF THE CROWD
180	You Should Be Loved / SIDE SHOW

The price of this publication includes access to companion recorded accompaniments online, for download or streaming, using the unique code found on the title page.
Visit www.halleonard.com/mylibrary and enter the access code.

Any Dream Will Do
from JOSEPH AND THE AMAZING TECHNICOLOR® DREAMCOAT

Music by ANDREW LLOYD WEBBER
Lyrics by TIM RICE

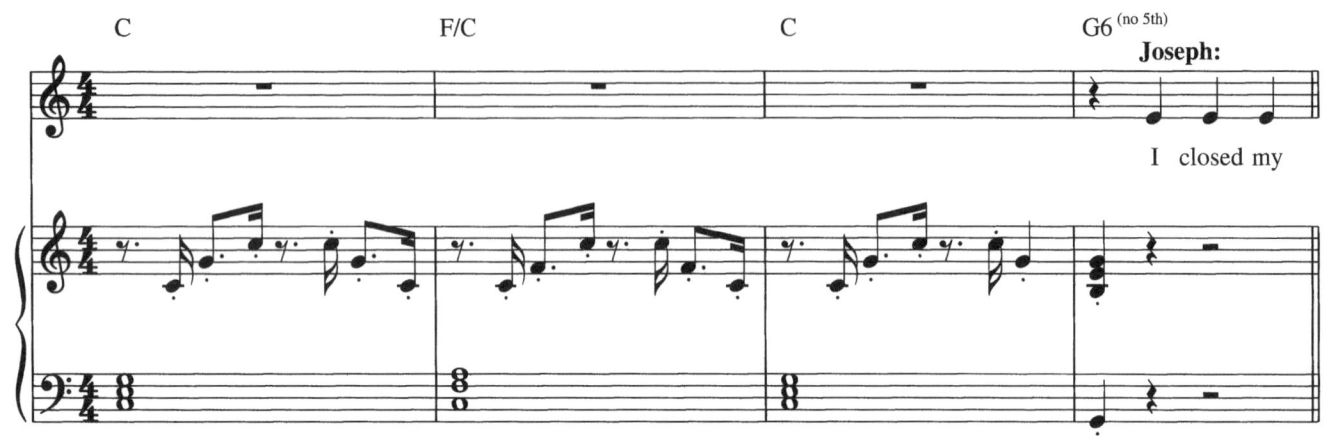
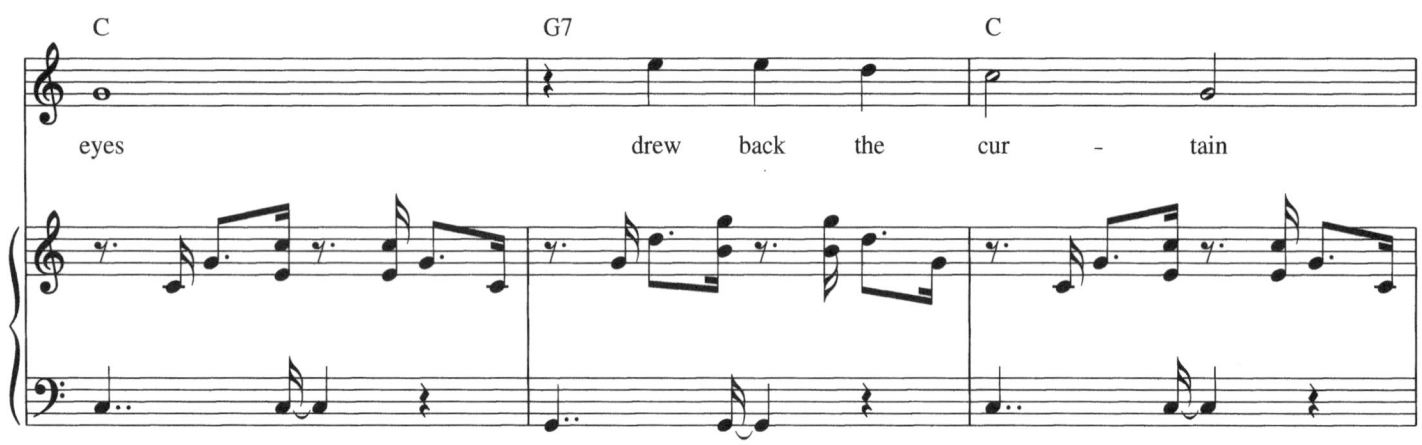
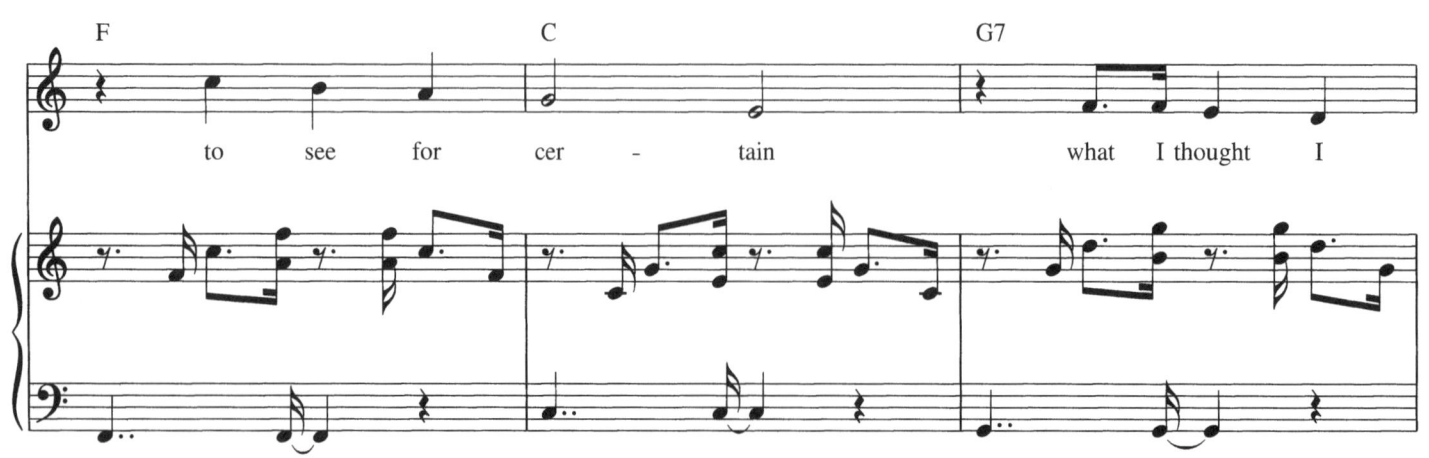

© Copyright 1969 The Really Useful Group Ltd.
Copyright Renewed
All Rights for North America Controlled by Williamson Music Co.
International Copyright Secured   All Rights Reserved

The Best Thing for You
from CALL ME MADAM

Words and Music by
IRVING BERLIN

Empty Chairs at Empty Tables
from LES MISÉRABLES

Music by CLAUDE-MICHEL SCHONBERG
Lyrics by HERBERT KRETZMER and ALAIN BOUBLIL

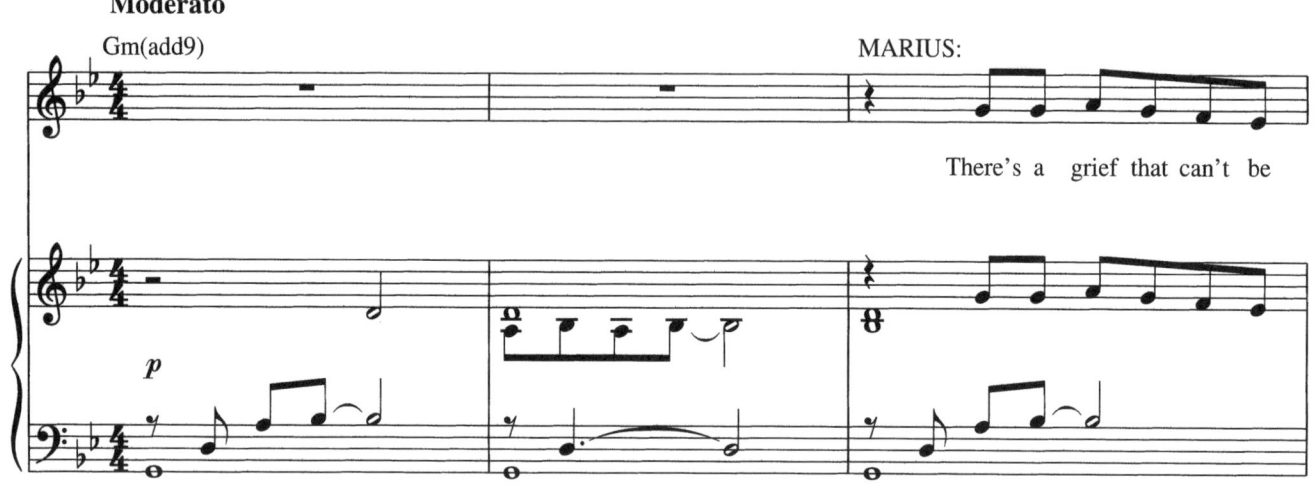

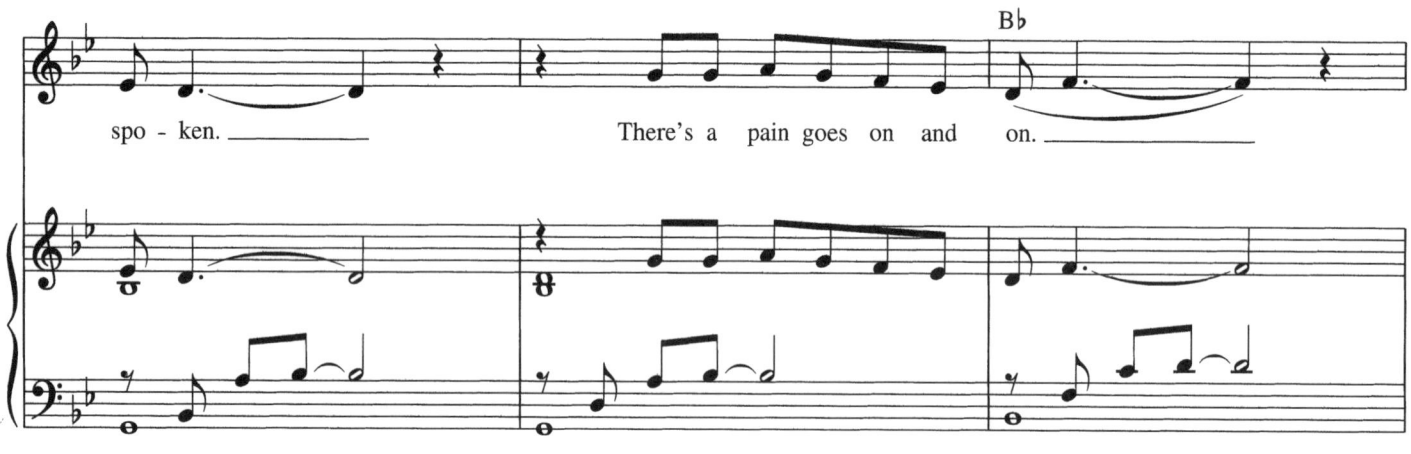

Music and Lyrics Copyright © 1986 by Alain Boublil Music Ltd. (ASCAP)
This edition Copyright © 2001 by Alain Boublil Music Ltd. (ASCAP)
Mechanical and Publication Rights for the U.S.A. Administered by Alain Boublil Music Ltd. (ASCAP)
c/o Stephen Tenenbaum & Co., Inc., 1775 Broadway, Suite 708 New York, NY 10019, Tel (212) 246-7204, Fax (212)246-7217
International Copyright Secured. All Rights Reserved. This music is copyright. Photocopying is illegal.
All Performance Rights Restricted.

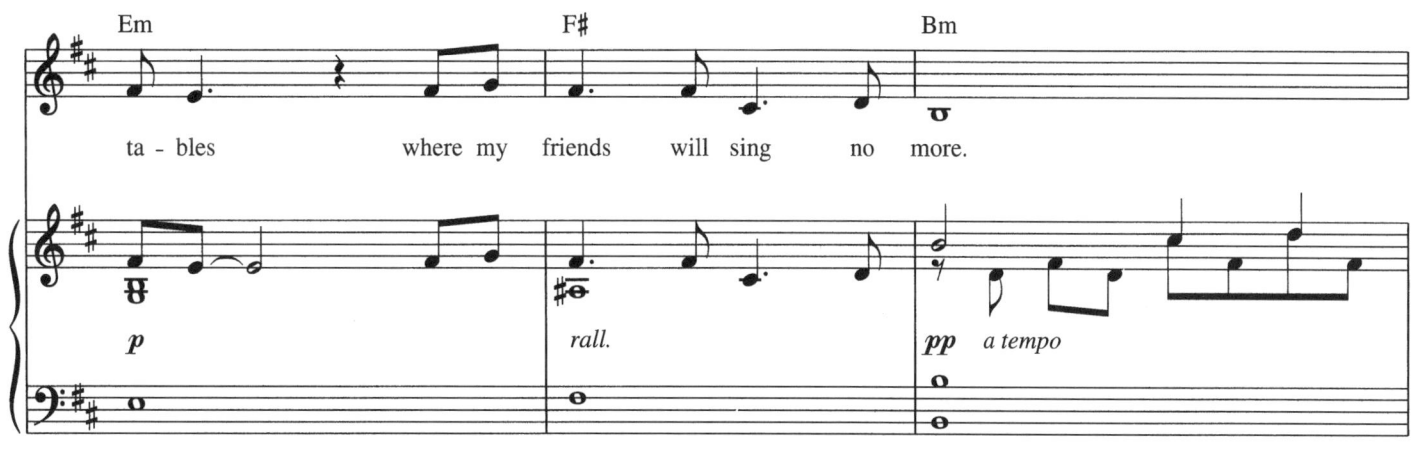

Everybody Ought to Have a Maid
from A FUNNY THING HAPPENED ON THE WAY TO THE FORUM

Words and Music by
STEPHEN SONDHEIM

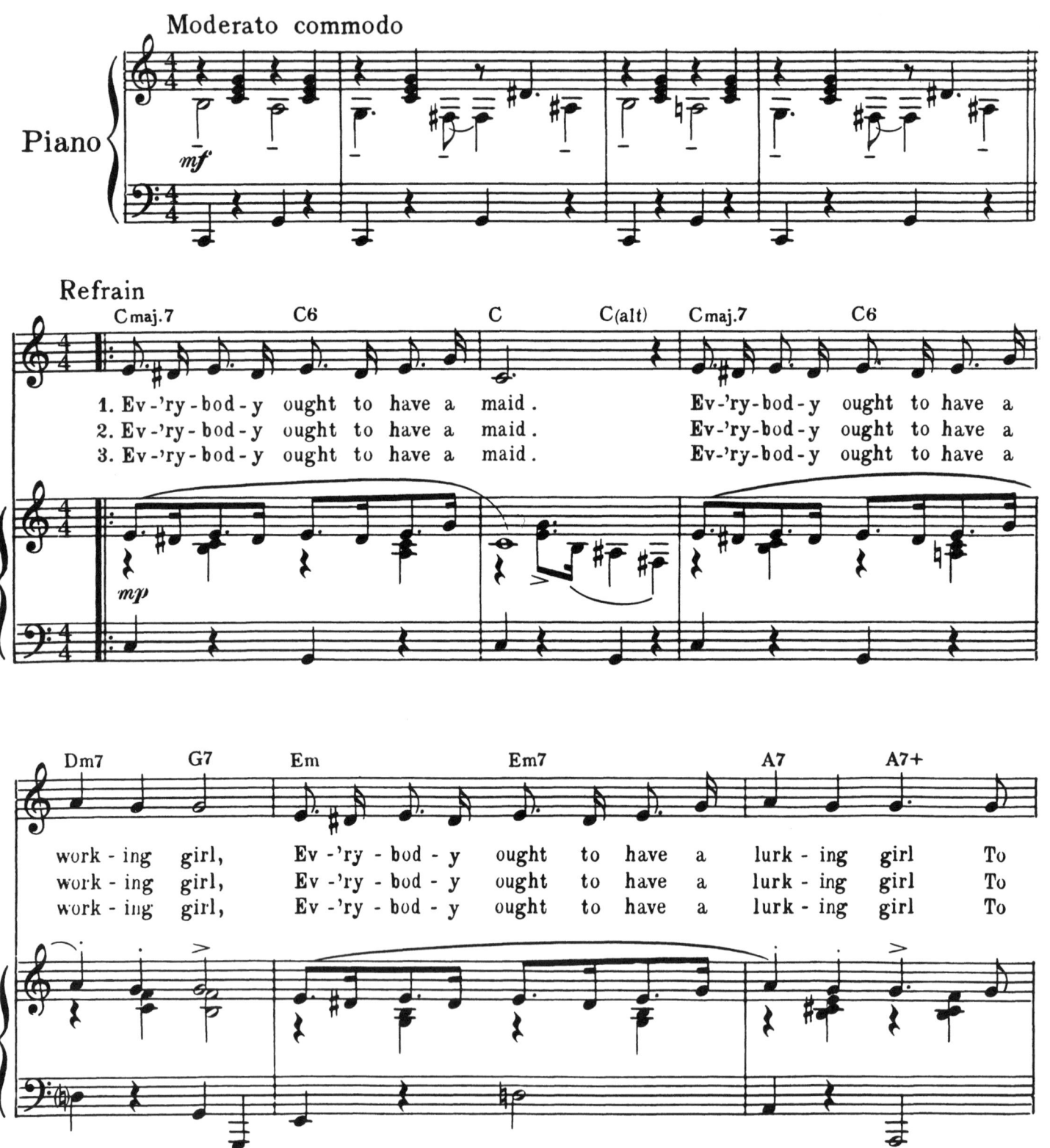

Copyright © 1962 by Stephen Sondheim
Copyright Renewed
Burthen Music Company, Inc., owner of publication and allied rights throughout the world
Chappell & Co., Sole Selling Agent
International Copyright Secured   All Rights Reserved

Ev'rything I've Got
from BY JUPITER

Words by LORENZ HART
Music by RICHARD RODGERS

34

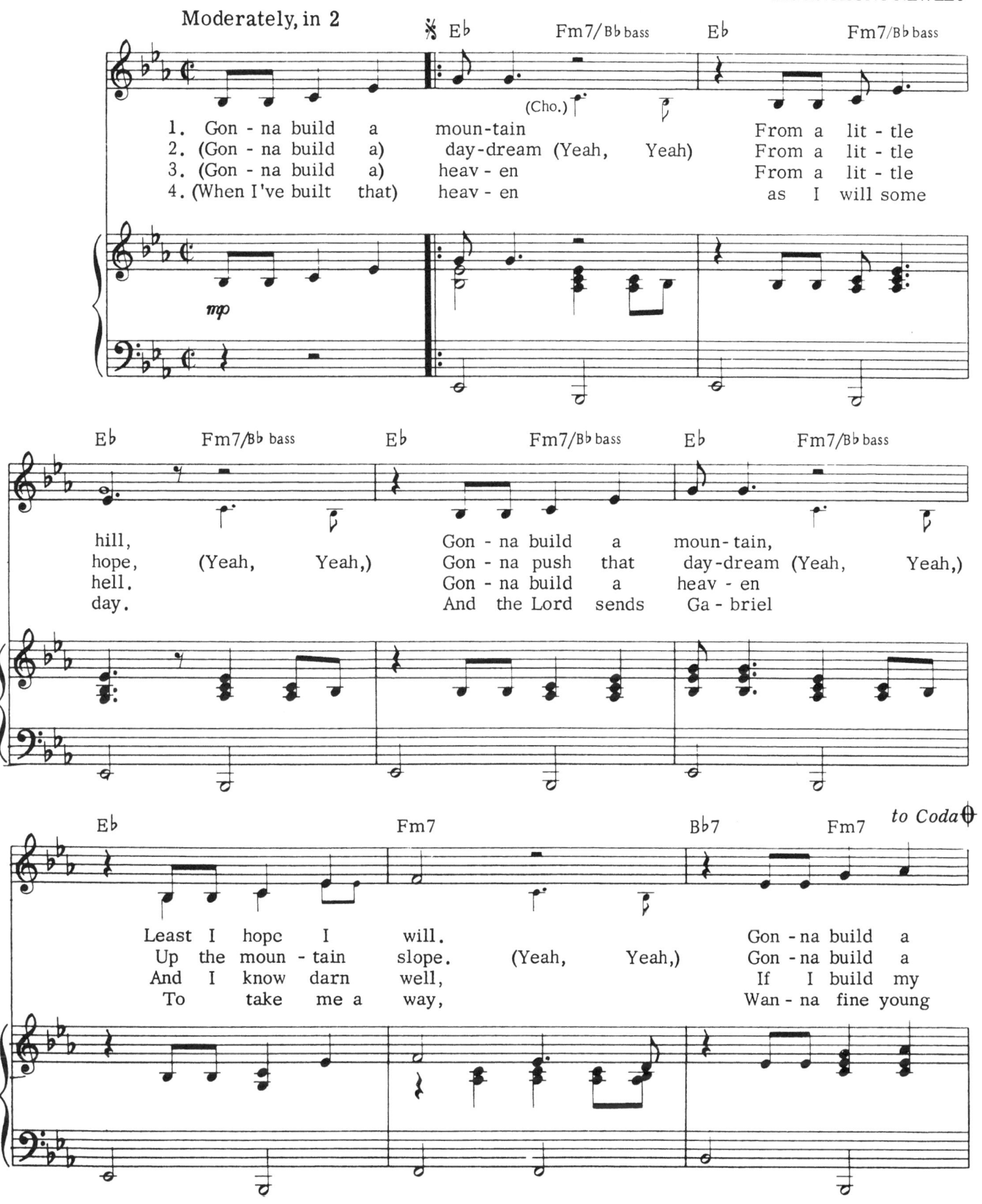

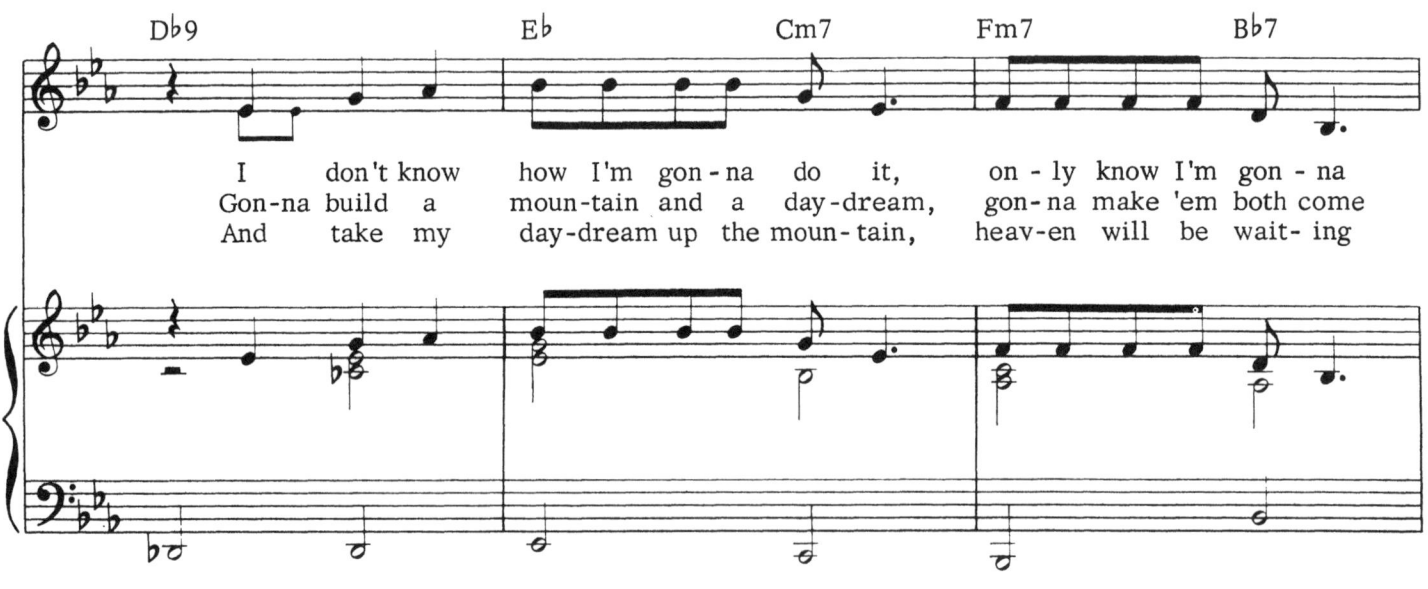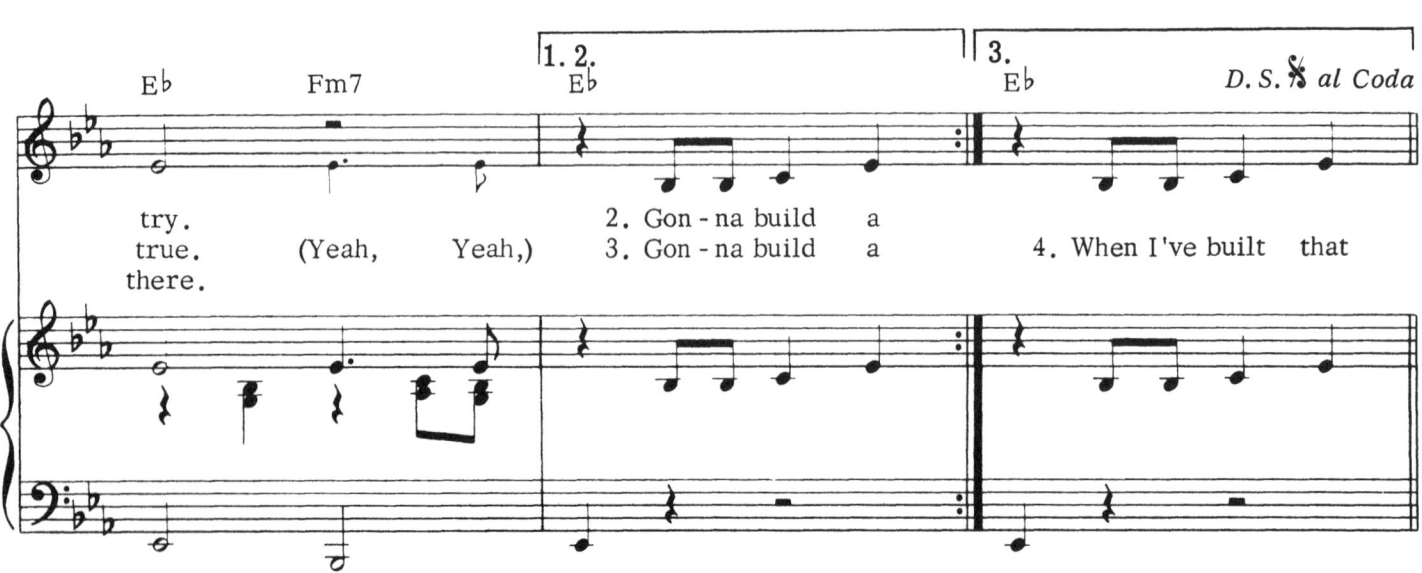

Gaston
from Walt Disney's BEAUTY AND THE BEAST: THE BROADWAY MUSICAL

Lyrics by HOWARD ASHMAN
Music by ALAN MENKEN

© 1991 Walt Disney Music Company and Wonderland Music Company, Inc.
All Rights Reserved   Used by Permission

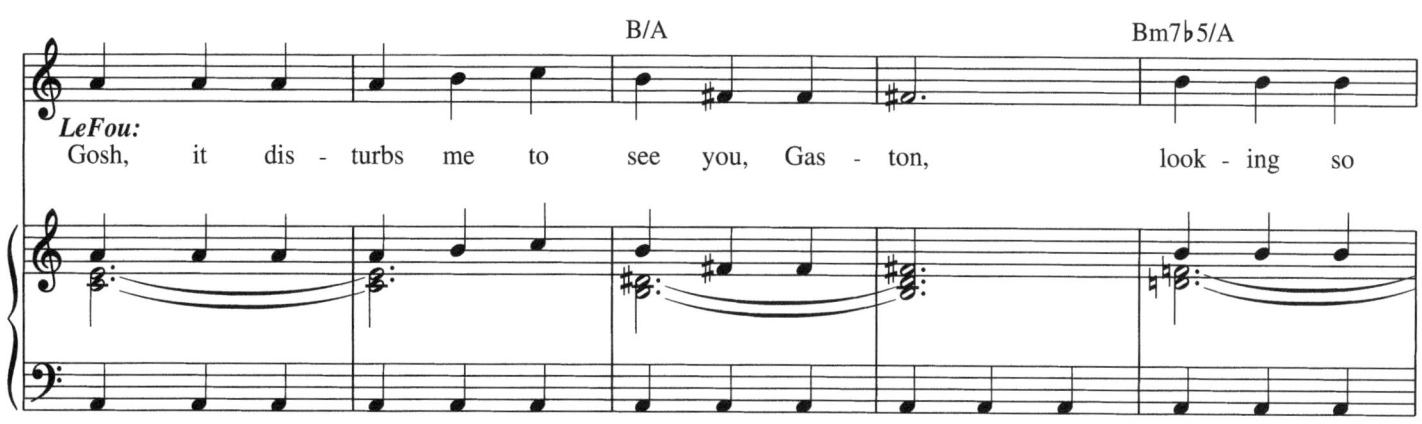

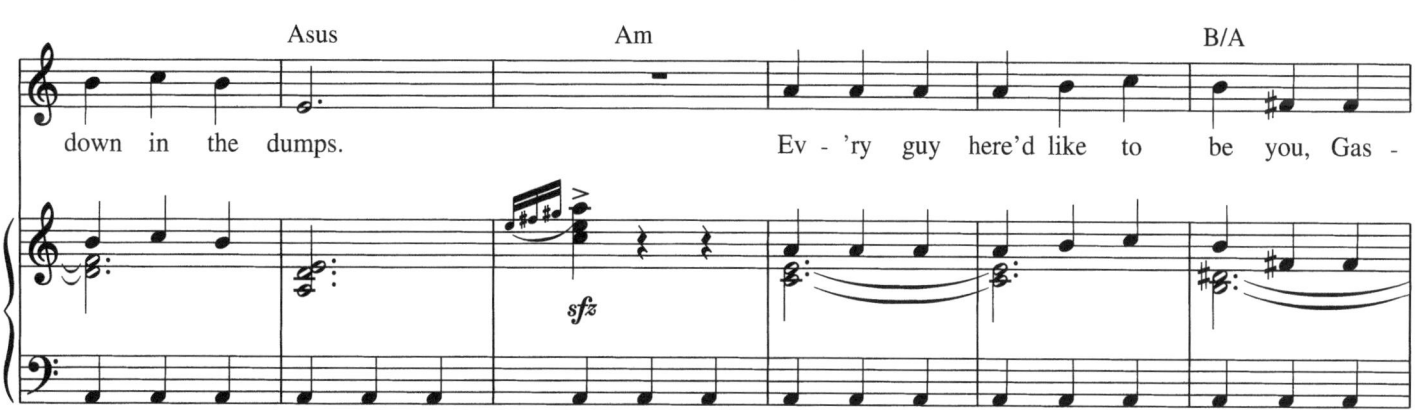

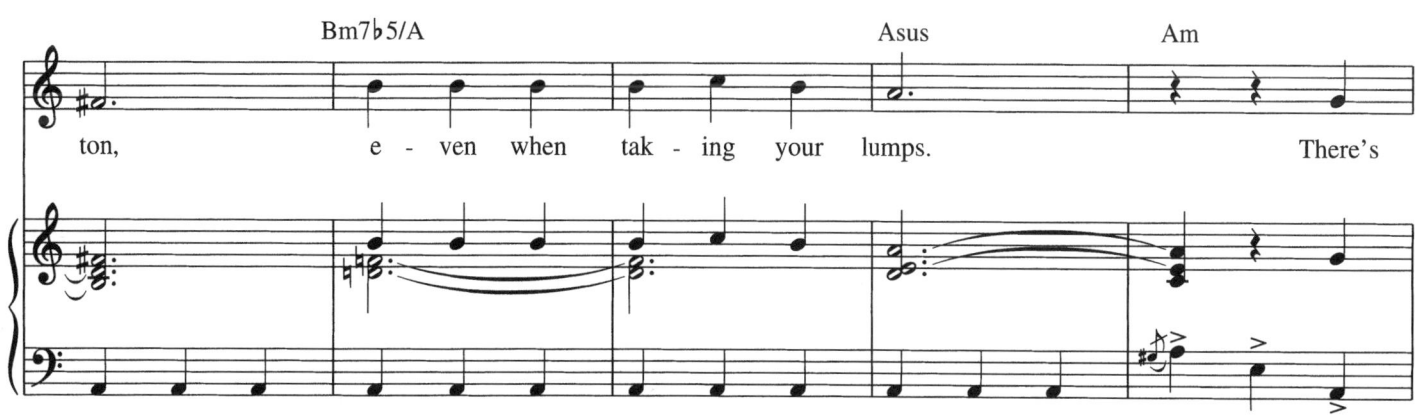

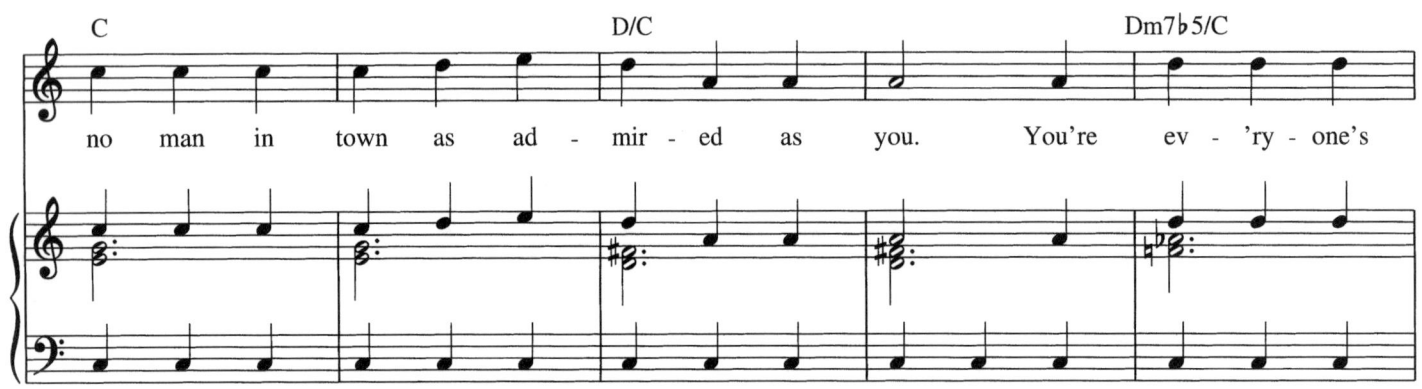
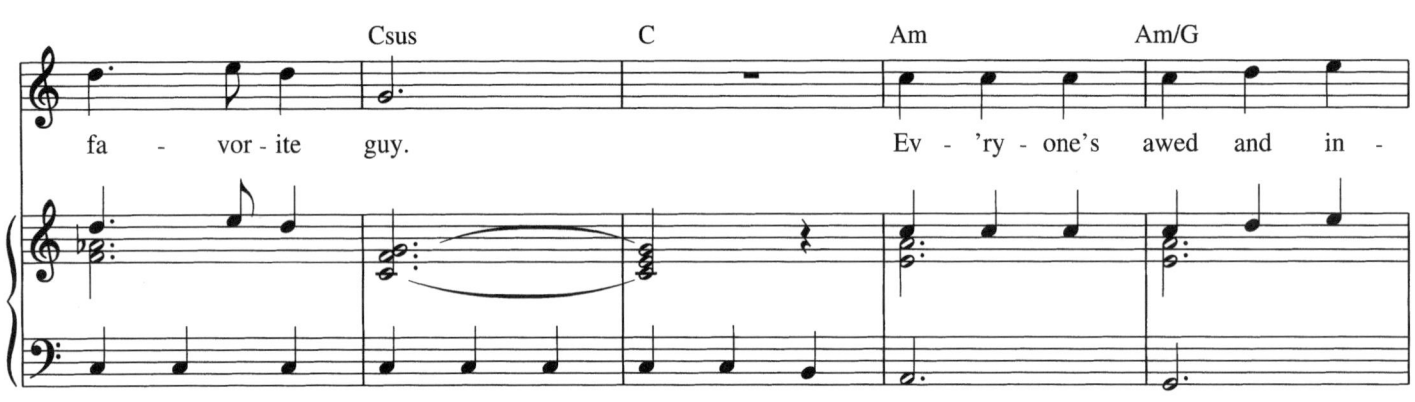
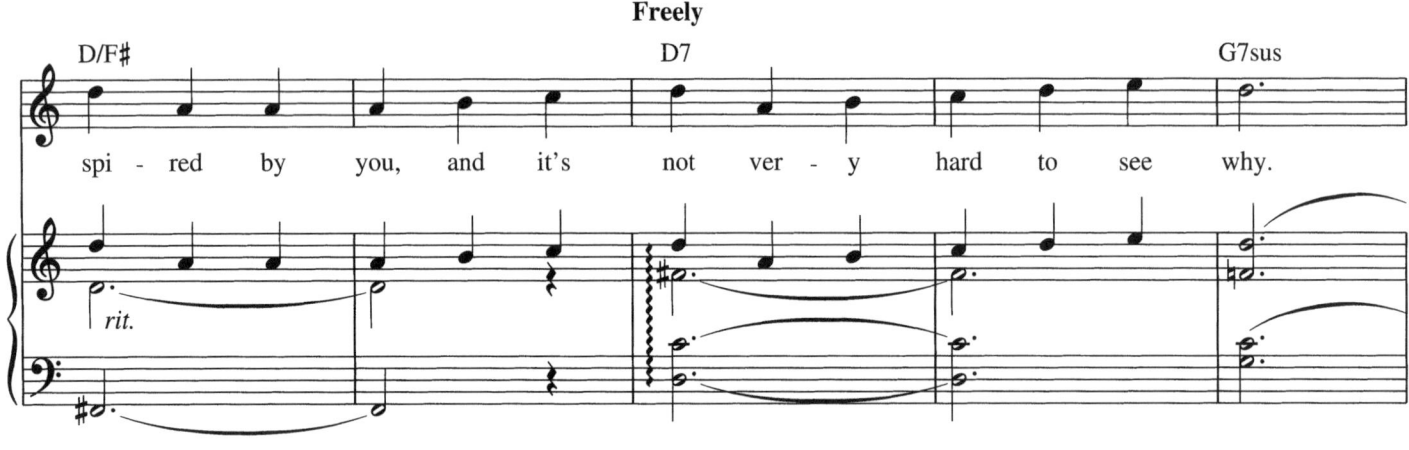
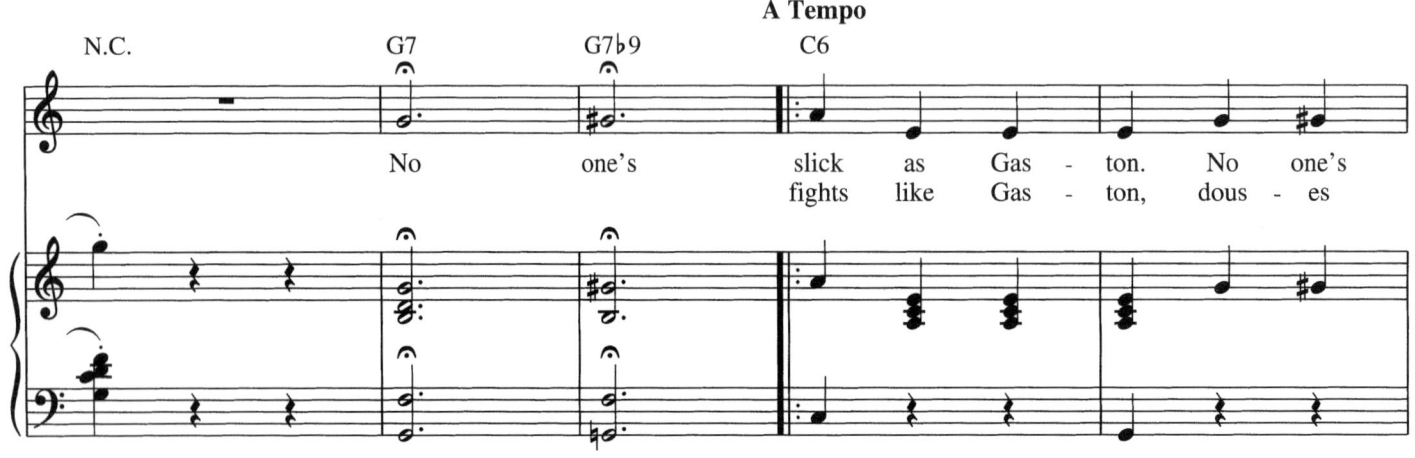

I Can't Stand Still
from the Broadway musical FOOTLOOSE

Words by DEAN PITCHFORD
Music by TOM SNOW

Copyright © 1998 by Ensign Music Corporation, Pitchford Music and Snow Music
International Copyright Secured   All Rights Reserved

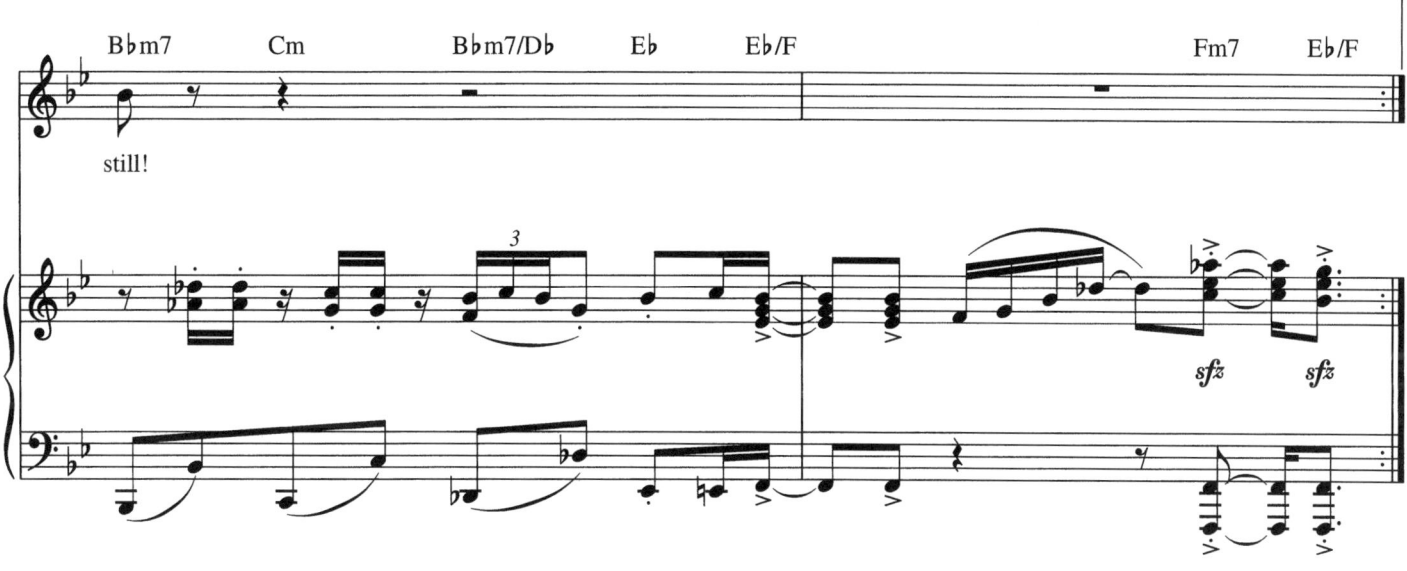

52

If I Can't Love Her
from Walt Disney's BEAUTY AND THE BEAST: THE BROADWAY MUSICAL

Music by ALAN MENKEN
Lyrics by TIM RICE

© 1994 Wonderland Music Company, Inc., Menken Music, Trunksong Music Ltd. and Walt Disney Music Company
All Rights Reserved Used by Permission

I'm a Bad, Bad Man
from ANNIE GET YOUR GUN

Words and Music by
IRVING BERLIN

Frank: I'm hon-ored, I'm flat-tered, This greet-ing real-ly mat-tered. This wel-come is grand but I'm real-ly con-cerned. I'm like your at-ten-tion, But this I have to men-tion, You're

Frank: For years I have yearned to play towns I could re-turn to, And "this may be it" from the way that you speak. I'm glad you're not fright-ened, The at-mos-phere has bright-ened, And

(After girl's chorus)

*For a solo version, omit the second ("Girls") verse.

© Copyright 1946 by Irving Berlin
Copyright Renewed
International Copyright Secured   All Rights Reserved

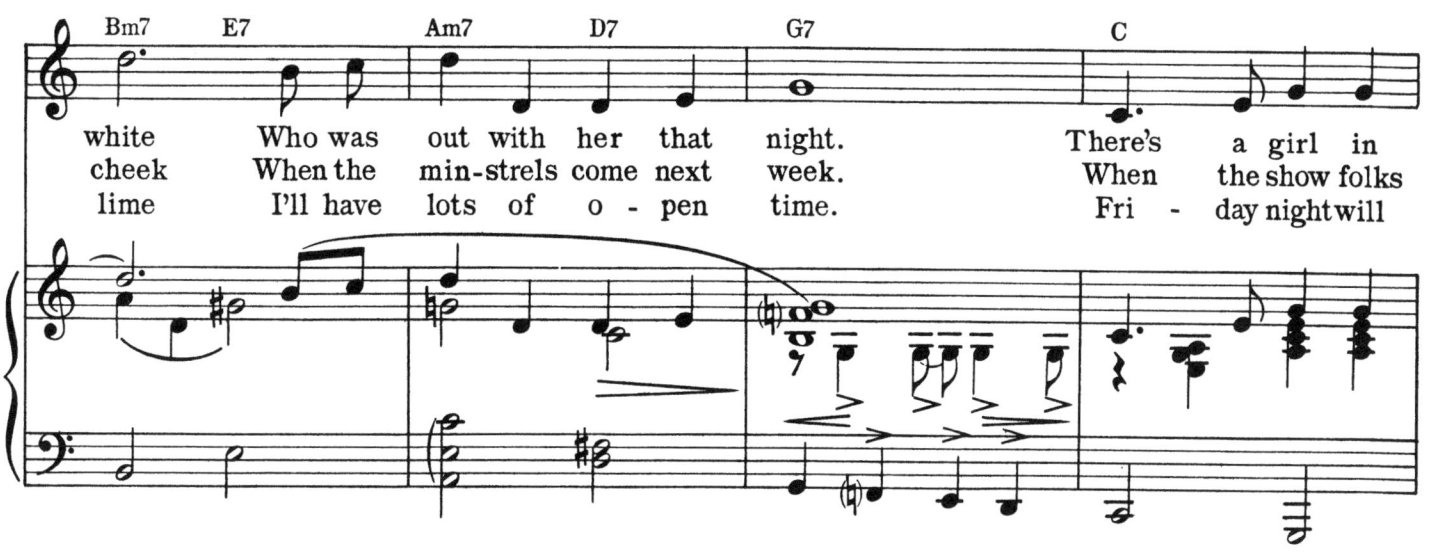
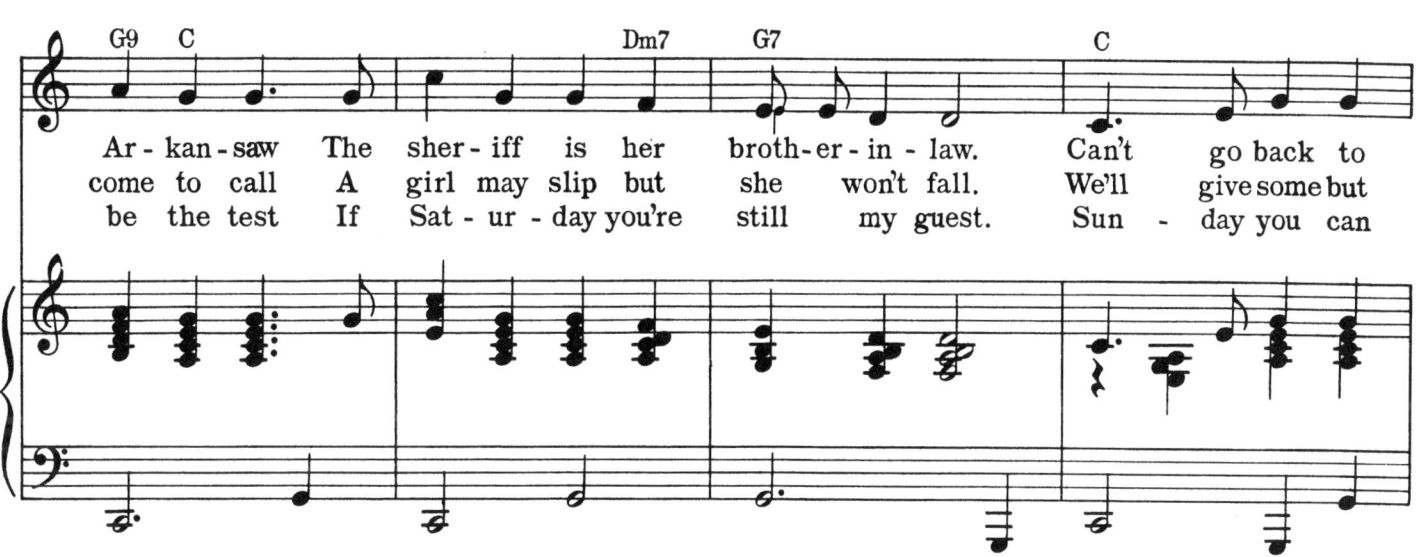

Isn't It?
from SATURDAY NIGHT

Music and Lyrics by
STEPHEN SONDHEIM

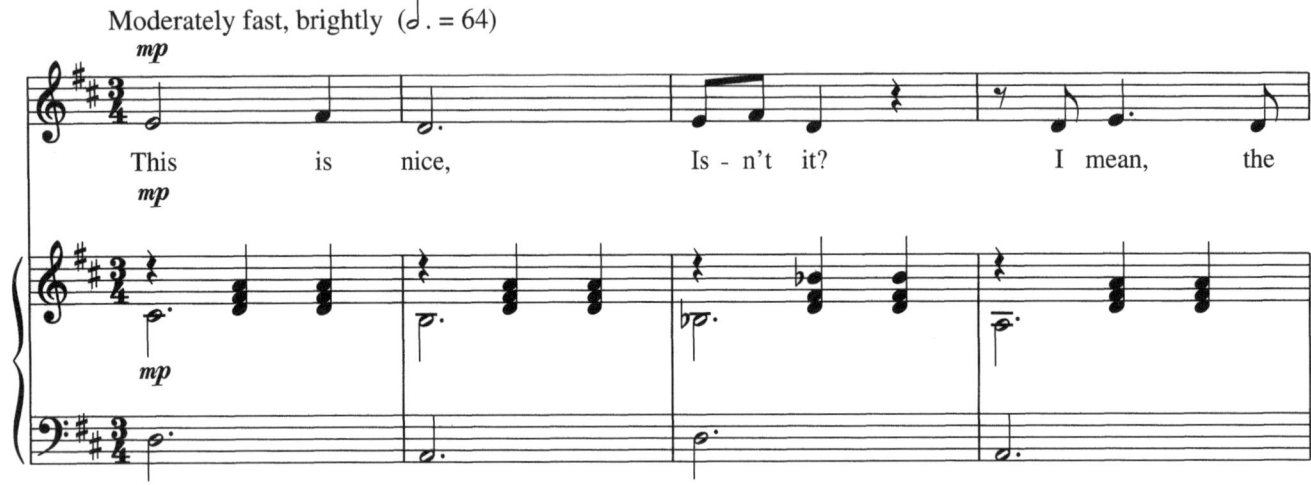

Copyright © 1984 by Burthen Music Company, Inc.
All Rights Administered by Chappell & Co.
International Copyright Secured All Rights Reserved

The Kite
(Charlie Brown's Kite)
from YOU'RE A GOOD MAN, CHARLIE BROWN

Words and Music by
CLARK GESNER

Quick, urgent

CB: Little more speed, little more rope, little more wind, little more hope. Gotta get this stupid kite to fly. Gotta make sure it doesn't snag, doesn't droop, doesn't drag. Gotta watch out for ev'ry little

© 1966, 1967 JEREMY MUSIC INC.
© Renewed 1994, 1995 MPL COMMUNICATIONS, INC.
All Rights Reserved

Kansas City
from OKLAHOMA!

Lyrics by OSCAR HAMMERSTEIN II
Music by RICHARD RODGERS

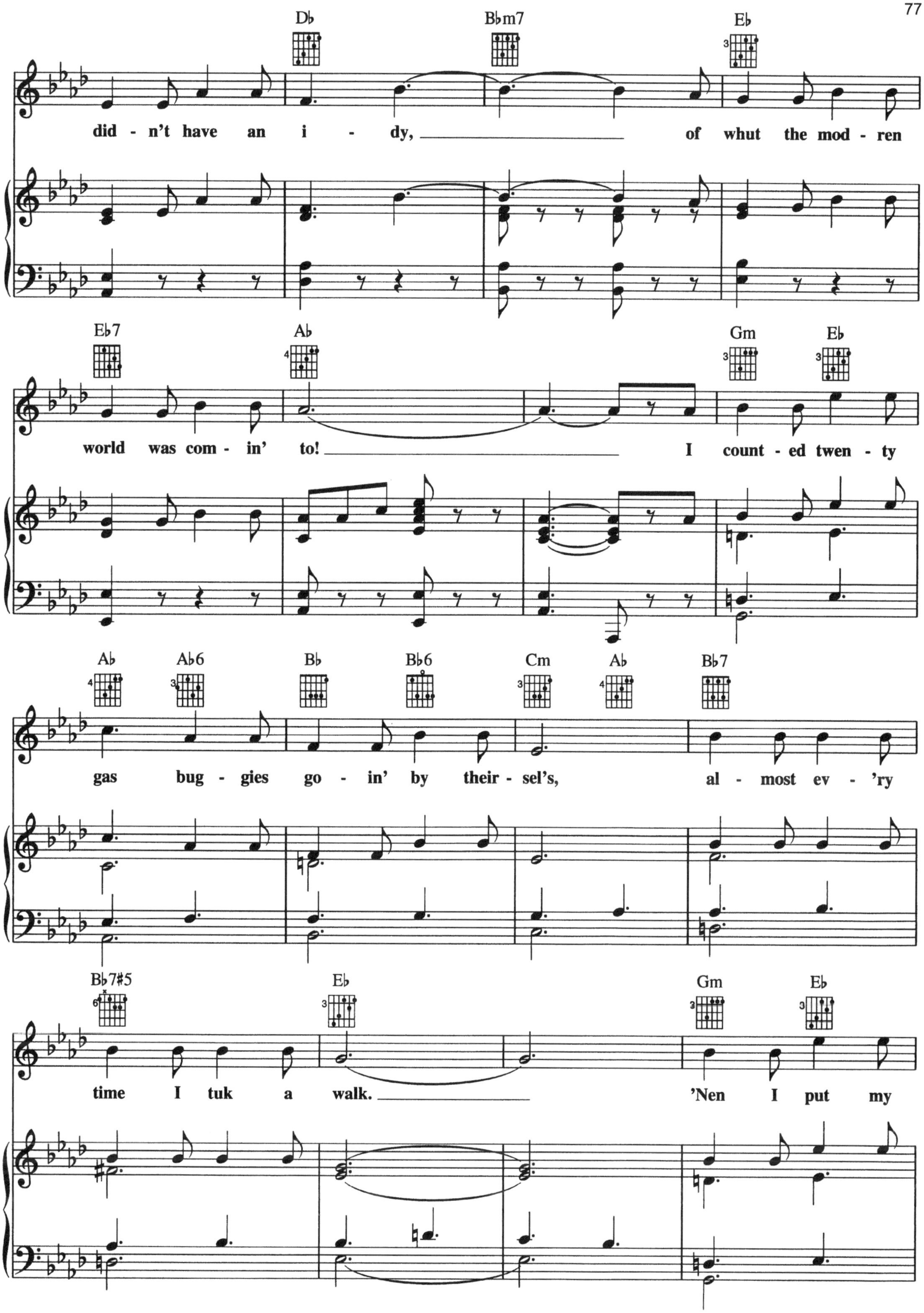
D♭ B♭m7 E♭
did - n't have an i - dy, of whut the mod - ren
E♭7 A♭ Gm E♭
world was com - in' to! I count - ed twen - ty
A♭ A♭6 B♭ B♭6 Cm A♭ B♭7
gas bug - gies go - in' by their - sel's, al - most ev - 'ry
B♭7#5 E♭ Gm E♭
time I tuk a walk. 'Nen I put my

Mama, A Rainbow
from MINNIE'S BOYS

Lyrics by HAL HACKADY
Music by LARRY GROSSMAN

Mama Says
from the Broadway musical FOOTLOOSE

Words by DEAN PITCHFORD
Music by TOM SNOW

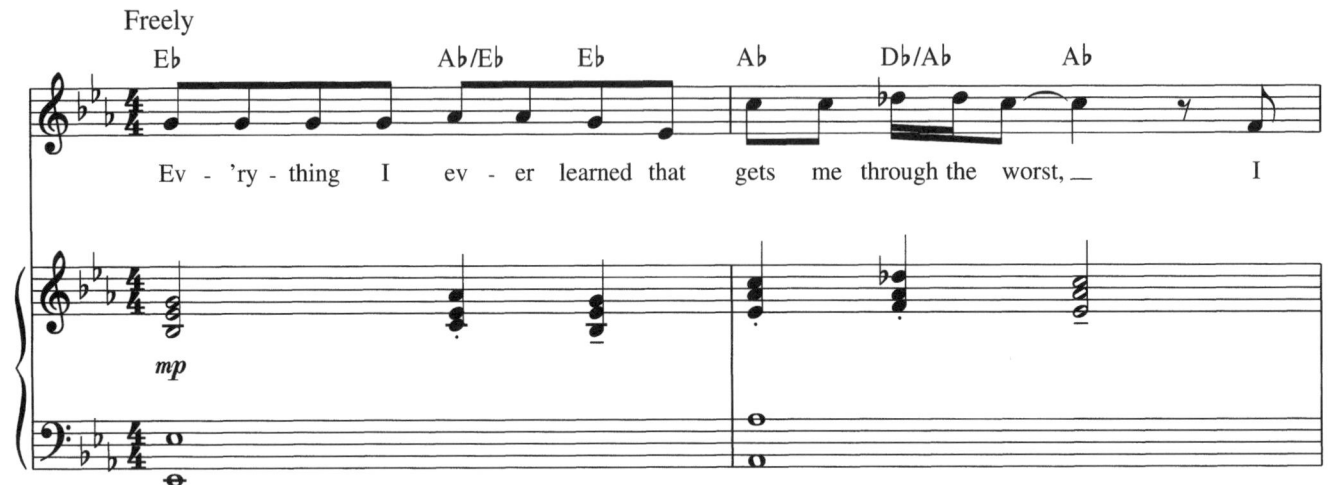

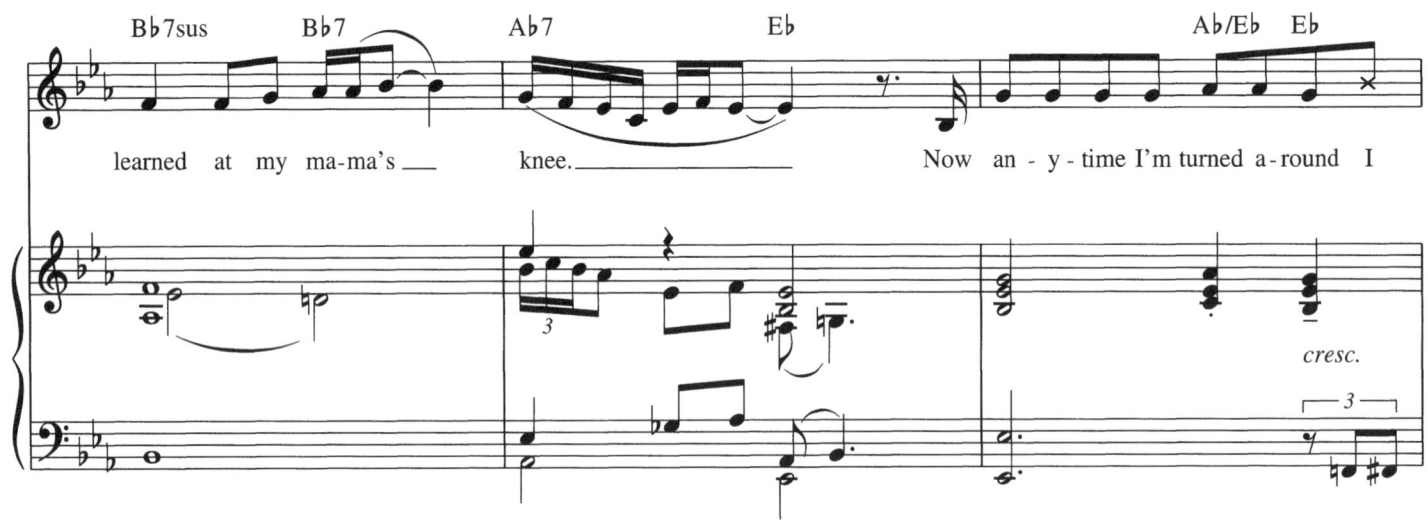

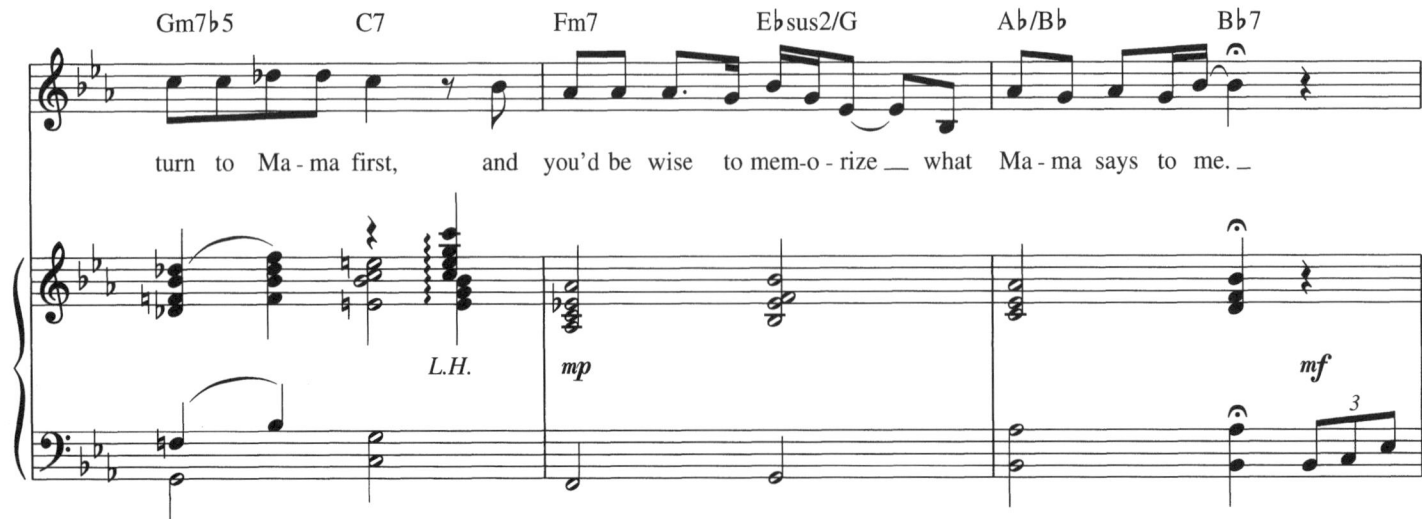

Copyright © 1998 by Ensign Music Corporation, Pitchford Music and Snow Music
International Copyright Secured   All Rights Reserved

Many Moons Ago
from ONCE UPON A MATTRESS

Music by MARY RODGERS
Words by MARSHALL BARER

Copyright © 1959 by Marshall Barer and Mary Rodgers
Copyright Renewed
Chappell & Co., owner of publication and allied rights throughout the world
International Copyright Secured   All Rights Reserved

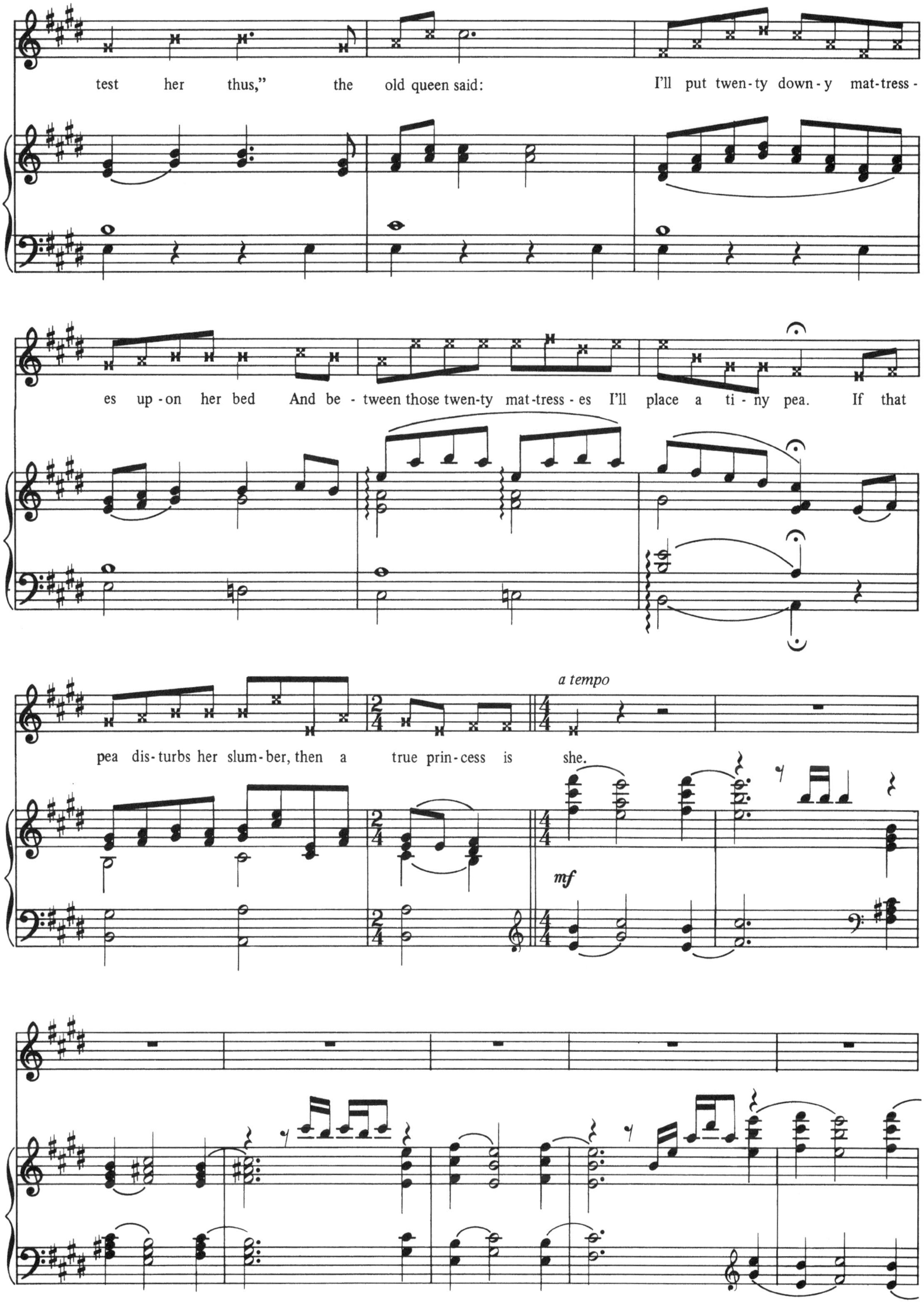
test her thus," the old queen said: I'll put twen-ty down-y mat-tress-
es up-on her bed And be-tween those twen-ty mat-tress-es I'll place a ti-ny pea. If that
a tempo
pea dis-turbs her slum-ber, then a true prin-cess is she.
mf

Movies Were Movies
from MACK AND MABEL

Music and Lyric by
JERRY HERMAN

My Name
from the Columbia Pictures-Romulus Film OLIVER!

Words and Music by
LIONEL BART

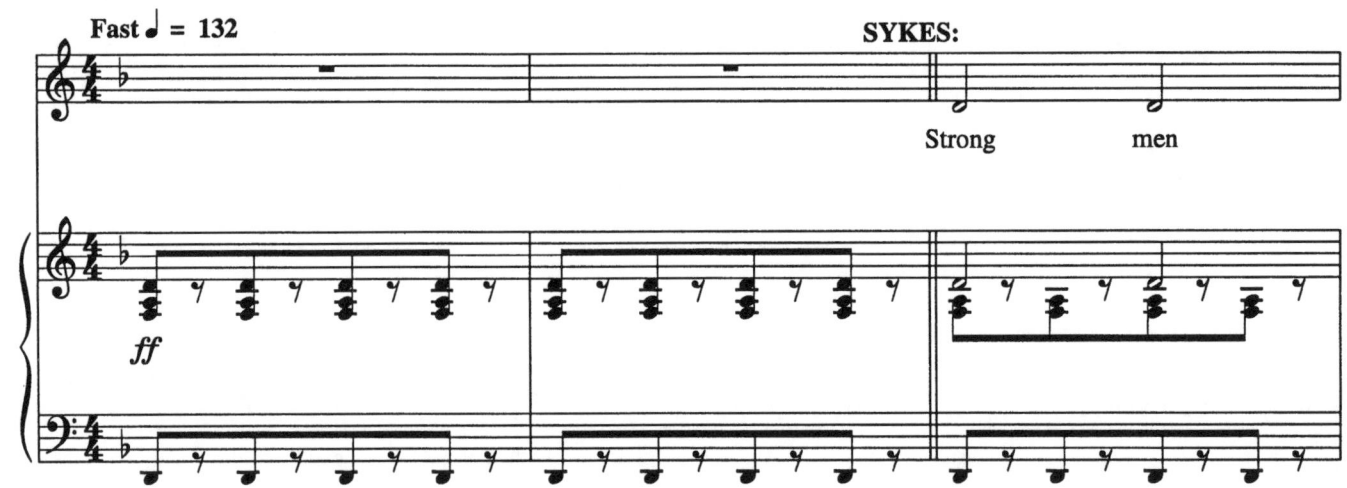

© Copyright 1960 (Renewed) Lakeview Music Co. Ltd., London, England
TRO - Hollis Music, Inc., New York, NY controls all publication rights for the U.S.A. and Canada
International Copyright Secured
All Rights Reserved Including Public Performance For Profit
Used by Permission

One Song Glory
from RENT

Words and Music by
JONATHAN LARSON

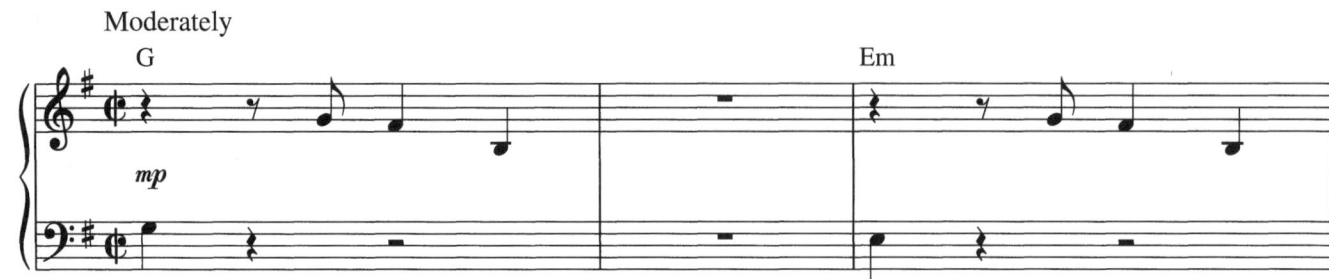

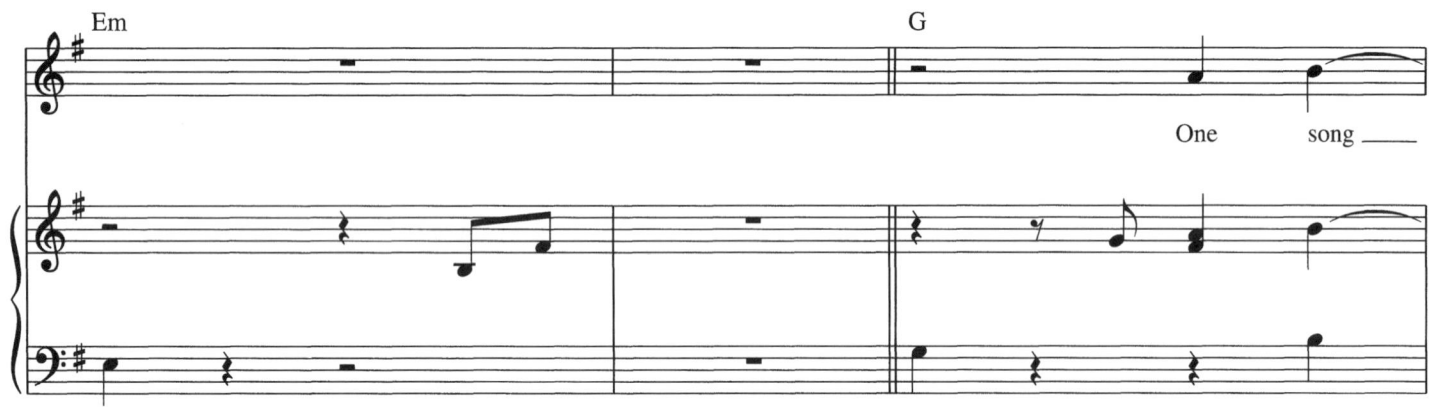

© 1996 FINSTER & LUCY MUSIC LTD. CO.
All Rights Controlled and Administered by EMI APRIL MUSIC INC.
All Rights Reserved   International Copyright Secured   Used by Permission

The Only Home I Know
from SHENANDOAH

Lyric by PETER UDELL
Music by GARY GELD

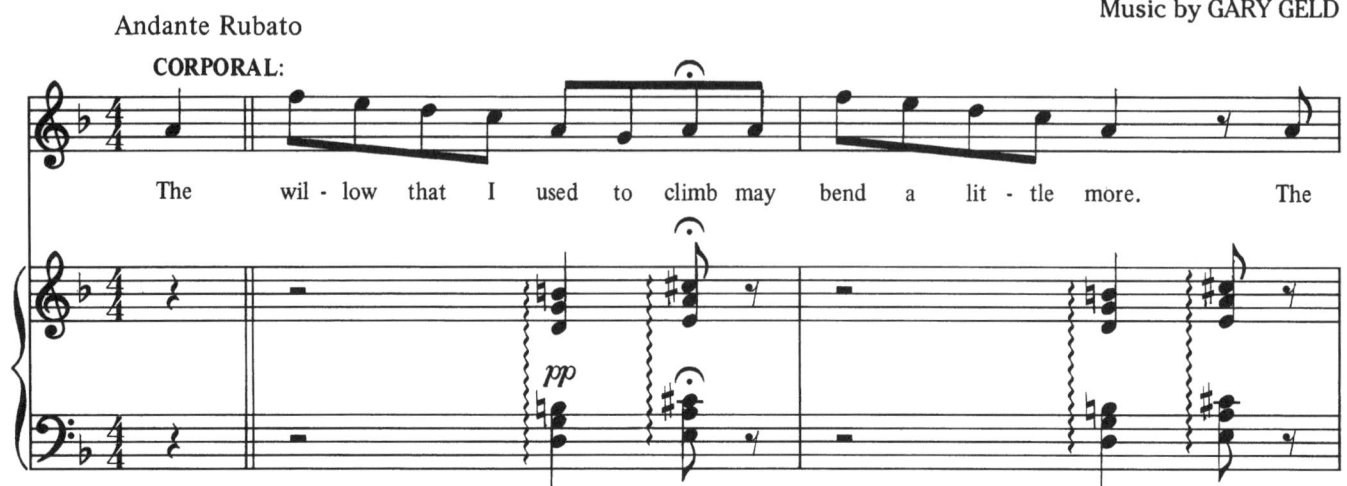

This song is sung with chorus in the show.

© 1974, 1975 GARY GELD and PETER UDELL
All Rights Controlled by EDWIN H. MORRIS & COMPANY, A Division of MPL Communications, Inc.
All Rights Reserved

Plant a Radish
from THE FANTASTICKS

Words by TOM JONES
Music by HARVEY SCHMIDT

Razzle Dazzle
from CHICAGO

Words by FRED EBB
Music by JOHN KANDER

Reviewing the Situation
from the Columbia Pictures-Romulus Film OLIVER!

Words and Music by
LIONEL BART

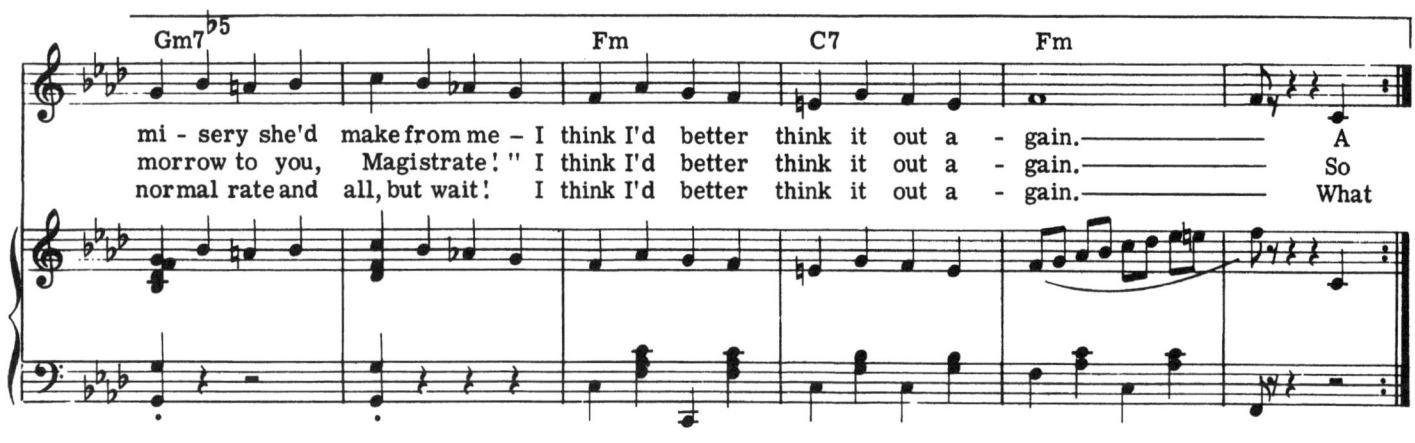

Soon It's Gonna Rain
from THE FANTASTICKS

Words by TOM JONES
Music by HARVEY SCHMIDT

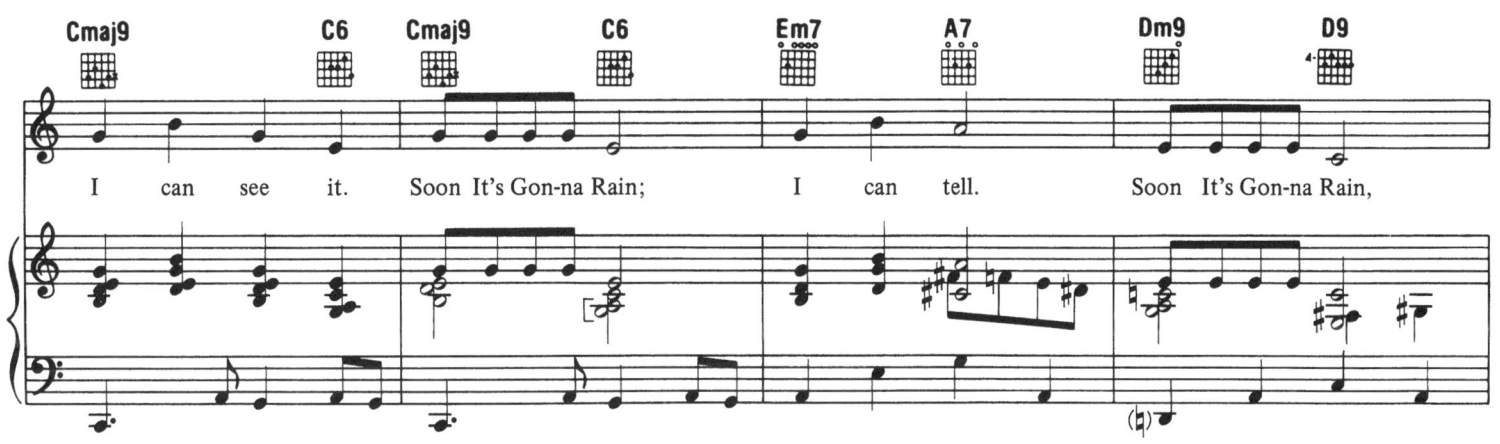

Copyright © 1960 by Tom Jones and Harvey Schmidt
Copyright Renewed
Chappell & Co. owner of publication and allied rights
International Copyright Secured   All Rights Reserved

Rumble, Rumble, Rumble
from the Paramount Motion Picture THE PERILS OF PAULINE

Words and Music by
FRANK LOESSER

Copyright © 1947 (Renewed 1976) by Famous Music Corporation
International Copyright Secured   All Rights Reserved

Waitin' for the Light to Shine
from BIG RIVER

Words and Music by
ROGER MILLER

Slowly (in a folk style)

A Wonderful Day Like Today

from THE ROAR OF THE GREASEPAINT—
THE SMELL OF THE CROWD

Words and Music by
LESLIE BRICUSSE and ANTHONY NEWLEY

Copyright © 1964 (Renewed) Concord Music Ltd., London, England
TRO - Musical Comedy Productions, Inc., New York, NY controls all publication rights for the U.S.A. and Canada
International Copyright Secured
All Rights Reserved Including Public Performance For Profit
Used by Permission

Where Was I When They Passed Out the Luck?
from MINNIE'S BOYS

Lyrics by HAL HACKADY
Music by LARRY GROSSMAN

Copyright © 1969, 1970 by Alley Music Corp. and Trio Music Company, Inc.
Copyright Renewed
International Copyright Secured   All Rights Reserved
Used by Permission

When I'm Not Near the Girl I Love
from FINIAN'S RAINBOW

Words by E.Y. HARBURG
Music by BURTON LANE

Copyright © 1946 by Chappell & Co.
Copyright Renewed
International Copyright Secured   All Rights Reserved

You Should Be Loved
from SIDE SHOW

Words by BILL RUSSELL
Music by HENRY KRIEGER

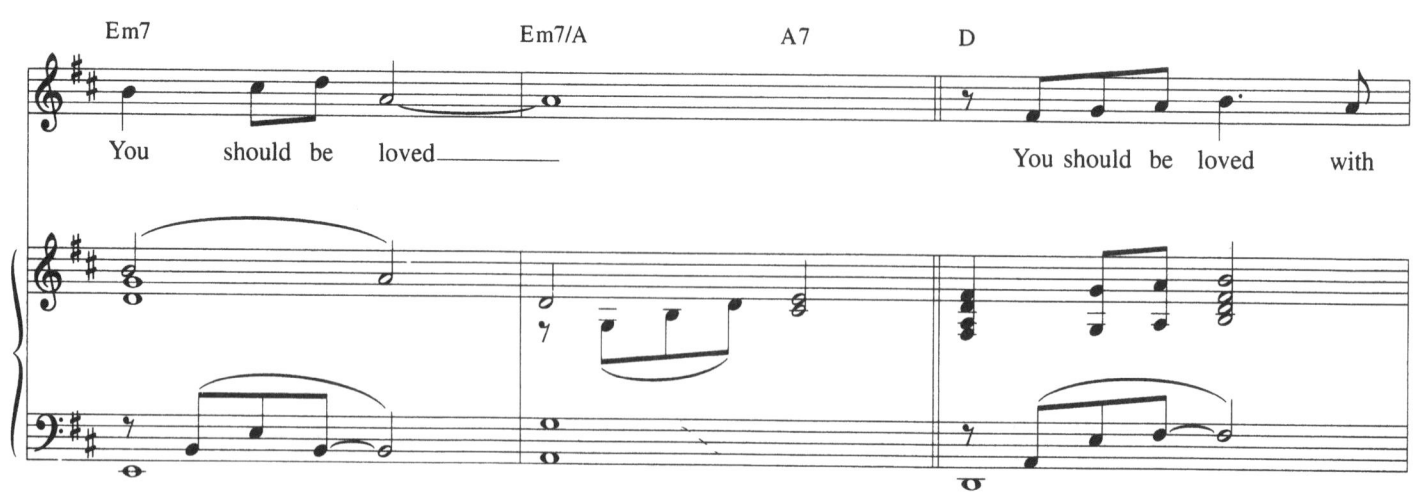

© 1994 MIROKU MUSIC (ASCAP)/Administered by A. Schroeder International Ltd., 200 West 51st Street, Suite 1009, New York, NY 10019
and STILLBILL MUSIC (ASCAP), 1500 Broadway, Suite 2001, New York, NY 10036
International Copyright Secured   All Rights Reserved